For

BARB
MOORE

NEVER ENOUGH

By Ronit M. Berman

Illustrated by Lyn Peal Rice

PETER PAUPER PRESS, INC.
WHITE PLAINS, NEW YORK

To my family, my friends, and my love, of whom I never have enough

Copyright © 1993
Peter Pauper Press, Inc.
202 Mamaroneck Avenue
White Plains, NY 10601
All rights reserved
ISBN 0-88088-764-8
Printed in Singapore
7 6 5 4 3 2 1

INTRODUCTION

Ever feel like there's never enough time to do all the things you want to do? Or maybe you never have enough quarters for the laundry? Or do you feel like the bear who can never get enough sleep—or honey?

We all come across things in our daily lives that there are never enough of! Before long, you'll be dreaming up your own additions to this collection of "never enoughs." But watch out, you may not be able to stop!

R.M.B.

NEVER ENOUGH

NEVER ENOUGH

Friends

Clean sheets

Gossip

Sunny days

NEVER ENOUGH

Gummy Bears

Hugs

Low calorie food that tastes good

Sleep

NEVER ENOUGH

Messages on your answering machine

Matching socks

Sex

Clean underwear

NEVER ENOUGH

Marshmallows on the sweet potatoes

Fresh cut flowers

Seats on the bus

Chocolate

NEVER ENOUGH

Monday night football

Paid sick days

Green lights

**Bathing suits that make
you feel attractive**

NEVER ENOUGH

Patience

Holes in one

Photos of your grand-children

Toilet paper

NEVER ENOUGH

Women in Congress

Edible airline food

Rainbows

**Chicken soup when
you're sick**

NEVER ENOUGH

Fresh milk

Gas in your tank

Volunteers to wash
the dog

People in love with you

NEVER ENOUGH

Snow on a ski vacation

Letters in the mailbox

Financial aid for college

Trees in the city

NEVER ENOUGH

Grateful Dead concerts

Umbrellas on rainy days

Professional recognition

Fish biting when you're fishing

NEVER ENOUGH

Shopping carts at the supermarket

Good new rock and roll

Full moons

Hours in the day

NEVER ENOUGH

Traffic-free drives home

Coffee that tastes the
way it smells

Pairs of eye glasses

**Personal conversations
with your father**

NEVER ENOUGH

Sets of keys to your house

Laundry detergent

Diamonds

Motivation to exercise

NEVER ENOUGH

Stars in the sky

Gifts on your birthday

Ice cream in an ice cream soda

Good men

NEVER ENOUGH

Job offers when you're unemployed

Good movies

800 numbers

Taxis on a rainy day

NEVER ENOUGH

Good restaurants

Checks in the mail

Skycaps at the airport

Help with the housework

NEVER ENOUGH

Pay days

Frequent flyer mileage

Daily calorie allowance

Honest mechanics

NEVER ENOUGH

Pantyhose without runs

Clean beaches

Counter space in the kitchen

Doctors who listen

NEVER ENOUGH

Bike paths

**Baby sitters on a
Saturday night**

Fizz in old soda

Comfortable shoes

NEVER ENOUGH

Working pay phones

White T-shirts

Freshly brewed coffee at the office

Chocolate chips in
chocolate chip cookies

NEVER ENOUGH

Window seats on
the plane

Pain-free dental visits

Checkout lines

People who agree
with you

NEVER ENOUGH

Rest stops on the highway

Interest in your bank account

Wishes that come true

Wind to fly a kite

NEVER ENOUGH

White meat turkey at Thanksgiving

Magic Johnsons

Clean coffee cups

Kisses

NEVER ENOUGH

People saying how great you look

Leg room on the plane

Ripe strawberries

Clothes that match

NEVER ENOUGH

Parties

Exits in a mall

Bathrooms when you have guests

**Home cooked meals
made by someone else**

NEVER ENOUGH

Toll-free roads

Filling in your sandwich

Laughter

**People who accept you
the way you are**

NEVER ENOUGH

Windshield wipers
that work

Whipped cream

Rent stabilized apartments

Bubbles in your bubble bath

NEVER ENOUGH

Raises

Time with your family

Customers who pay
on time

Respect from your children

NEVER ENOUGH

Department store sales

Plants that can survive without water

Time

Happy people

NEVER ENOUGH

Birdies

Postage stamps

Space on the shelf for new books

Stalls in the ladies' room

NEVER ENOUGH

Clean bathrooms at gas stations

Love, sweet love

Naps

Springtime

NEVER ENOUGH

Good horoscopes

Quarters for the laundry machine

Encouragement

Lunch hours

NEVER ENOUGH

Winning lottery tickets

Beautiful views

Mornings when nothing aches

Money

NEVER ENOUGH

Last pages of a good book

Vacation time

Days when everything goes right

Foot massages

NEVER ENOUGH

Time to read the paper

Friends with vacation homes

Tapes for the VCR

Powder on the ski slopes

NEVER ENOUGH

Coffee breaks

Minutes left on the
parking meter

Shopping days before
Christmas

Time to yourself

NEVER ENOUGH

Return on your investments

Blessings

Peace in the world

Happy Endings